MW00949394

Mr. Christopher Maxwell

Thomas – The Informant

There was a difference, I saw it

as soon as I saw the body. The

FBI agent that showed him to

me was one that I was

suspecting. There was

something to this murder that

wasn't spelled upon the wall.

They brought me in to be one

of the many to find out just

what it was that was wrong. My

research took several weeks,

but after that time I was sure I

had come to the conclusion

that was sure to upgrade me.

The next morning I showed up

to the precinct, as soon as I

entered the building I was

bombarded but, I can't believe

what you've done, and we

never suspected you. For the next three hours I was held in the interrogating room drilled with all types of questions like where were you on the night of the murder? No matter what I said they wouldn't listen to me.

My conscious is clean I kept saying. Until that moment. One of the sergeants went to set his glass of water down on the table, ad I just happened to notice that he had the same tattoo that was on my mind when I first entered the

building in the morning. For the

next couple moments I not only

proved my innocence but

proved that the particular

sergeant was guilty of cold

blooded murder.

I spent the next couple of months in the Bahamas. The warmth that permeated from the room next to mine, was lovely. I could always count on it too. Like, if I was having a bad day or something blew up in

my chemistry class, or all

together my mother died, I

knew that no matter what that

night I was going to be cuddled

up against something warm.

The Bahamas though was the

shit. I went wakeboarding,

which I had never done before,

but I figured I'm in the

Bahamas, and since you only

live once, I wake boarded.

When we returned safely home

in the Carolinas, North Carolina,

I decided to take a nap against my warm wall. Though I never did find out what made that wall so warm. I never asked. I just kept it a secret. I had a job and I loved what I did, however I always wanted to do my own

FBI reporting behind the walls so to speak. I wanted to become a writer. I told my wife about it one night, she seemed indifferent, well have to uproot the children, little johnnie will never make it at a new school he has special needs. What about Jim, his older brother that kid can make it in any high school that we send him to. You could home school little Johnnie. We have some savings saved up that will get through for a few years until I can get

my feet wet. Most people jump

out of planes, Jennie from

Forrest Gump did it from a

balcony in her hotel room. But

is it possible to do it in the

comfort of your own home

with your children watching on,

wife crying to never Neverland.

Common said the Future is

here Today. Yesterday I

received a text message from

the millennials, I have Trump

syndrome I have this and I have

that . Maybe you shouldn't

fight an answer at the bar every

Saturday and Sunday night.

Maybe you should look within

yourself and spell Facebook

instead of Siri. There is a was

out of this, you have to let me

help you, I am there now let me

get you there too, take my

hand. The next few weeks were

hard I had to put down the

beer and pick up a gallon of

water, I had to think to myself

which one is healthier beer or

water? There always was the

coffee that one depleted me

from my aqua but didn't get me

drunk, was usually my

hangover cure, but not this

particular day. You see I went

out to the club, and just club

made me realize high prestige and if my wife worried about me cheating on her I best wear a suit. Asked her the next day and she said she didn't mind it, so I went out and bought a $500.00 Armani suit. There wasn't much on this earth that

pained my wife until one day in

may, my son johnnie came

home with a big gash on his

right knee, exclaiming owiie

mommy "fix me." She did the

best she could, and saved it

with a little bit of water and

some love kisses, in our house

we called them love kisses

because of how well they heled

wounds. Lots of them healed

quickly.

If you dream in your own visionaries and not in another's, your doing well for yourself. If you dream within the realms of another man's jurisdiction you need to see a shrink. There are may places around the world that would gladly kill Batman's parents again outside a Ballet on there way home and none would be the wiser. Therefore there is only one thing to say about life and that is just keep going, "Auggies STD."

Christopher Maxwell Thomas.

My wife says to me she says I

feel like were in some weird

science fiction through the

third act and we are not even

on Abilify, have you studied

that one yet honey, remember

our roles it was your job to

study the the different

mechanisms of these new anti-

psychotics, I know babe that

was the next one on my list, ok

I says the next half begins.

After the things that me and

my wife do together we always

get back to business and talk

about some of the major things

in life that way we don't et

blindsided by life. I was sitting

in the den when I noticed a

white robe enter the room the

light was dim so I didn't notice

it was my wife, she had a stack

of papers in her hand. I asked

her what they were for, she

simply said that she was

starting a new journal. O I said,

I didn't think much of it. MY

wife always had a secret o two

that she kept from me. I was

hesitant but I was able to

mention the writing career

again, this time she said with a

smile on her face she would

support me in whatever

endeavor I chose.

Made in the USA
Las Vegas, NV
21 February 2021

18253992R00017